INSPIRATION

for the Heart

Also in this series:
Inspiration for the Soul

INSPIRATION

for the Heart

KATE MARR KIPPENBERGER

EXISLE
PUBLISHING

First published as *Soul Food for the Heart* 2007
This edition published 2015

Exisle Publishing Limited,
'Moonrising', Narone Creek Road, Wollombi,
NSW 2325, Australia
P.O. Box 60-490, Titirangi, Auckland 0642, New Zealand
www.exislepublishing.com

A CiP record for this book is available from the
National Library of Australia.

ISBN 978 1 921966 90 3

Text design and production by BookNZ
Cover design by Dexter Fry
Printed in China

This book uses paper sourced under ISO 14001 guidelines
from well-managed forests and other controlled sources.

10 9 8 7 6 5 4 3 2 1

Reason

There will be times in our life when we deal with a person who refuses to see reason, behave logically or accept the facts. There may be many reasons for this, but the most common is that they have let their emotions get in the way. While people who display these behaviours are very frustrating to deal with, we need to realise that it's going to be difficult, if not impossible, to reach an understanding or agreement. Rather than attempt to achieve something that is unlikely to happen, we might be best to avoid the frustration and not engage them.

Healthy Living

Every day we receive information about healthy living. For many of us, to live a healthy lifestyle would involve changing a great deal about the life we lead. We don't exercise enough, we don't eat 5+ fruit and veges a day, we have a tendency to get stressed, we work too hard, we don't take time out for ourselves, and so on. Beginning a healthy regime can seem overwhelming, so we don't change anything to improve our lifestyle. Yet we shouldn't let this put us off. All change is made by doing one thing at a time, and rather than feeling bad about being unhealthy and overwhelmed at the scale of change required, think of one healthy thing you can do today. It's a start.

Live The Moment

Some find it hard to enjoy the moment – they tend to look forward to it or think fondly of it afterwards. These people are most comfortable thinking 'in their heads'; this takes less energy than being present in the moment and savouring it. To enjoy the moment we have to clear our heads of thoughts and focus on what is happening. This takes discipline and concentration, but the result is to be truly engaged in life as it is happening now. Don't miss out on the fun, joy and happiness that is only truly present in the moment.

Emotions

If we have a problem with someone else's behaviour and we want to talk to them about it, we'll achieve a lot more if we keep our own negative emotions out of the situation. People don't respond well to negative emotion. It can make them feel defensive. It can also set the tone for the confrontation and rather than resolve the issue, the negative emotion can become the focus of the interaction. If we keep our focus on the behaviour we're concerned about and communicate in a manner that doesn't reveal negative emotion, we're more likely to be heard and more likely to have the issue sorted out.

Busy Busy Busy

If we agree to undertake many different tasks, the energy and effort we can put into any one of them will be reduced. The more we have to do, the less we can concentrate fully on completing one thing well. While we might feel good about being able to say 'yes' to everything we're asked to do, if we take on too much we run the risk of not doing anything particularly well. This might be necessary if there are lots of things that must be done. But under normal circumstances taking on too much will have a negative impact on the quality of what we can achieve.

Television

It's easy to get into the habit of watching television every night – especially during winter when the nights are cold and dark. Yet there are many other things we could be doing instead. If watching television has become a habit, we're unlikely to think of alternatives. The problem with this is that we might be missing out on something much better: we could be spending our evenings doing something more stimulating and fulfilling. The best way to find out what we could be doing is to have a night off watching TV – we'll soon occupy ourselves with something.

Time Management

If today is looking extremely busy and stressful, turn it into something that can be managed. If we let our minds become overwhelmed by what's in front of us, we're not likely to be very productive, so break the day up into manageable 'chunks'. Everything that we need to do can be broken up into a series of tasks. If we begin our busy day by tackling a small and manageable task, we'll get started, we'll not be overwhelmed and we are more likely to achieve what we hope to achieve. Your day is ahead of you and is yours to manage to your advantage.

Meaning

If we're able to find meaning in the tasks we do, we can always create a sense of fulfilment within ourselves. But when it comes to the tasks we don't want to do, more often than not we find ourselves thinking of all the things we'd rather be doing instead of finding meaning in what we're currently doing. This tends to make time drag, but more importantly we're missing the opportunity to gain fulfilment from what we're doing right now. There will always be tasks that we have to do. We can either waste the time or put some effort into finding some meaning, and therefore some fulfilment.

Every Day

Our life largely consists of the 'stuff' we do every day. There are times when we have special days — we might be on holiday, for example, or it might be our birthday — but on the whole these days are far fewer than the normal day-to-day life we have. For most of us it's not feasible to make 'every day a holiday', but that doesn't mean that we can't put effort into making every day as good as it can be. It's normal to feel an anticlimax after one of those special days, but why not make our usual day-to-day life something to be enjoyed also?

Burning Bridges

We never know what the future holds. Think about your own life now — are there people you never thought you would interact with and things you never thought you would be doing? We don't know who we're going to run into or what we're going to need from various people in coming years, so it's important that we don't 'burn bridges'. Not only is it highly negative to treat someone in a manner that they're unlikely to forgive (or forget) but you might be doing yourself a disservice in the future. If you do what's 'right' today, it's unlikely to come back to haunt you.

Change

We are creatures of habit and tend to like things that are familiar to us. The familiarity brings a sense of comfort and security. We may also get some self-esteem from familiar aspects of our life. Change can have an impact on us at many levels. Obviously negative change is unpleasant and it's not a stretch to see how this affects us, but positive change can have an impact also. Even if we want the change to happen, the fact that we're changing an aspect of our life can take some adjustment. It's important to realise this and take extra care with ourselves at all times of change.

Ourselves

It's important that we do nice things for ourselves from time to time. It may be taking time out to be alone, having a relaxing bath, cooking ourselves a nice meal, going for a walk, or having fresh flowers around the house. It doesn't have to cost money to make ourselves feel good. The fewer pennies you have to spend, the more creative you need to be. If we consider our own happiness important, we'll do what it takes to make us happy. Thinking about what we need to do for ourselves is often the biggest hurdle — then we just need to do it.

Intentions

If someone wants to do something, they will try really hard to make it happen. If they don't want something to happen, they will try hard not to make it happen, or not try hard to make it happen — there is a subtle difference. If we're not trying hard to make something happen, it might be because we don't really want it to happen. That reality might not be acceptable so we make out we do want it to happen, yet don't do anything to assist. It is helpful to realise this for ourselves and in others.

If someone else says they want something to happen yet they don't try to make it happen, there's a chance they don't really mean what they're saying. The old maxim 'actions speak louder than words' applies.

Plan

There will be times when we will be more efficient if we take time to plan what we're about to do. An example of this is writing a list for the supermarket. Without one, we'll probably be walking down every aisle looking at every product to jog our memory – and then we'll probably forget something. But if we have made a list, we can focus on getting exactly what we need, we won't forget anything and we won't buy unnecessary items. Writing a list does take some time at the beginning, but it could save time (and money) later on, so it's worth it.

Chill Out

Life is not meant to be taken too seriously. Situations come and go and they may be positive or negative. Enjoy the positive ones and learn from the negative ones, but don't let them get you down. Because we're so used to letting negative experiences get us down it may seem difficult not to take them so seriously, but it's a choice. Just because we've learned one way to respond, doesn't mean it's the only way for us to react. It will surely take a lot of extra effort to respond differently from normal, but the outcome will be worth it.

Unresolved Conflict

Unresolved conflict between two people can become like a 'dead elephant' between them. Think about what a dead elephant would look like in such a situation: it's huge, it's very difficult to move, it's unpleasant, and when the two people look at each other all they see is the dead elephant. When we think about disagreements in this way, it always makes sense to try and ensure that we resolve conflict when it arises.

If the unresolved conflict turns into a 'dead elephant', we will have far more unpleasantness to contend with in the future than we have now.

Anger

Like happiness, anger comes from within, yet we often try to externalise the cause so that we avoid having to take responsibility for the feeling.

If we avoid responsibility and the feeling doesn't arise (as in happiness) or does arise (as in anger) we can then blame others for this.

The difference is that a life without happiness is sad but a life with anger is destructive. Blaming others for our anger has far greater consequences for us than blaming others for our lack of happiness. Therefore if we're angry, we owe it to ourselves to take responsibility for the feeling and make it go away.

A Two-way Street

The way we think about people influences the way we behave towards people. The way we behave towards people influences the way they react to us, think about us and behave towards us. Therefore the way we think about people can influence the way we are treated in return. We tend to focus on the way we're treated more than the way we treat others, but if you're not being treated as well as you'd like, consider how you're thinking about and treating them. You may be eliciting unfavourable behaviour by your own attitude. You may be creating the very behaviour you would like to stop.

Assumptions

We tend to make assumptions about intentions and motivations from witnessing someone's behaviour, yet our chances of making a correct assumption are average to poor. First, behaviour doesn't always mirror intentions. Secondly, we could be interpreting the behaviour incorrectly. Thirdly, we're making assumptions about the person's intentions and motivations based on what we know — which might not apply to the person in question. While we all make assumptions based on behaviour because it's the most obvious tool we have, it's important to realise that we might not always be right. So be wary of launching into action or accusation as a result of your own assumptions.

Responsibility

We are responsible for our own life. If we constantly blame others for what has happened to us, we're not likely to move forward and do what is necessary to have a fulfilling life. While we may feel justified in blaming others for what has happened to us, it's not going to have a positive effect on us or our life going forward. No one else can make our future as fulfilling as we can make it — if we take responsibility for doing so. If we don't, we will have no one else we can blame.

Time

If there's something that you know you have to do, be wary of putting it off. The way we live our lives these days, we're very busy and time can pass us by easily. Before we know it a week or a month has passed. It can be scary and disappointing to think about what we could have achieved over that time had we just got on and done what we knew we had to do. If you think of something that has to be done — do it. Otherwise, you may be so busy you won't get to thinking about it again for a long time.

Effort

If we put in little effort, we're likely to get little in return — whether it is from other people or in achieving goals we set ourselves. If we put in lots of effort, we're not only more likely to benefit from the effort in real terms, but we can end up feeling really good within ourselves. Putting in effort requires time and energy in the moment, and when we're present in the moment, we benefit. If our effort doesn't yield the results we'd hoped, the personal benefits from putting in that effort and from living in the moment will still be felt.

Thoughts

Our minds can only focus on one thing at a time. If we think about negative things all the time, we need to consider why that is. Has it become a habit? Are there positive things we could think about but we've become used to focusing on the negative? If we keep our minds active by thinking about a variety of subjects, chances are we're less likely to be consumed by negativity. Yet if we let our minds always turn to negative matters and don't find other things to think about, we're likely to feel the effects of constant negativity.

Unhappiness

If we're unhappy, it can be difficult to be around happy people. We can feel as though their happiness accentuates our unhappiness. However, it's a misconception to think that we'll feel better if surrounded by unhappy people. The negative energy that comes from unhappy people cannot create a positive feeling in us. While being around other unhappy people might make us feel more 'normal', it certainly will not make us feel happy. If we want to feel happy, it's happy people we should endeavour to be around. Having said this though, no matter who we're around, if we don't take responsibility for our own happiness it won't happen.

Healthy Eating

When we eat healthy food, we feel good both physically and mentally. When we eat 'junk' or processed food it can have a negative impact on the way we feel physically and mentally. Moreover, if we constantly eat 'junk' food, we can forget what it feels like to have abundant energy and a positive outlook. Feeling less than our optimum can become our new norm. The only way to know how good we can really feel is to give our bodies a break: exercise more and eat healthily. The positive difference you notice might be enough to motivate you to continue with the healthy regime indefinitely.

Role Models

It's important for our children to have as many positive role models as possible in their lives. If they turn to other people for different aspects of their learning, and those people have our children's best interests at heart, then it's important for us as parents to support them. We can't always be everything to our children, and if we find they go elsewhere for support, help or advice, this doesn't detract from our relationship with them.

If we think about what's best for our children, and there are others around us who do the same, our children will certainly benefit.

Control

It's important that we feel in control of our life and of ourselves. There are many things that happen in life that we can't foresee but which have an impact on us. However, there are also things that impact on us that we can control, such as the food we eat, how much exercise we do, how much time we give ourselves each day, whether we think positively or negatively, the activities we choose to undertake. Don't forget that we always have the choice to be in control of ourselves, even at times when things are changing around us.

Your Best

It's important that you always try to do your best. If you know you did your best, it makes it easier to live with a negative outcome because you couldn't have done any better. Knowing you did your best can relieve any frustration caused by thinking 'if only…'. By always trying to do your best you're more likely to achieve your true potential. However, if you find that your best is not getting you the results you want, consider how you can improve 'your best' by working on your attitude, knowledge, experience and skills. Your best and the results you can achieve are within your control.

Fulfilment

A lot of us are searching for the 'thing' that's going to make us feel fulfilled. We know that we're not totally fulfilled with what we're doing now, so we're trying to find things that will make us feel that way. We might do it by surrounding ourselves with nice things, buying a new car, changing jobs, changing partners, going on holiday, etc. If we neglect the essence of ourselves — our soul or spirit, we're likely to feel unfulfilled. If we spend our time trying to 'fix' this neglect with external things, it's not likely to help. Taking care of who we are is the important thing.

Goals

We set goals and strive to achieve them because we believe that in doing so we'll benefit in some way. Setting a goal means striving to achieve a future outcome, yet circumstances do not remain constant and we are continuously changing also. Occasionally, therefore, achieving a goal we set ourselves in the past is not going to benefit us. Just because we spent time working to achieve the outcome doesn't mean we must stick with it, especially if it's no longer working for us. Don't be afraid to change tack if you find that your previous plans are not eventuating as you had hoped.

Vulnerability

When people feel vulnerable they are likely to take action to avoid feeling vulnerable in the future. People tend to feel vulnerable when they are in a situation that is beyond their control and they're relying on that situation to provide them with something they value. There are always alternatives to feeling vulnerable and usually it's not until we feel this way that we can see the alternatives. It's of little use trying to make someone else feel vulnerable by threatening to take something away that they value, as they're likely to find an alternative that eliminates our opportunity to do so.

Imagination

It can be easy for us to let our minds run wild and create all sorts of reasons why things happen. This can be particularly damaging if we tend to imagine the worst. For example, if you haven't heard from a friend in a while, don't assume it's because of something you've done; it's more likely to be because they're busy. If you start to think it's about you, you can become defensive about something that doesn't exist and create problems the next time you are in touch. Rather than create problems where they don't exist, try focusing your thinking on something more constructive.

Victim

If we're going through a time when things are happening to us that seem to be beyond our control, it's important to keep our thinking in perspective. It can be easy for us to believe we're completely at the mercy of events, and so relinquish what control we do have — our own reaction to what is going on. If we focus on the things we can't control, we're not thinking about how we can make the best of the situation or what we can learn from it. Falling into the trap of feeling like a victim is not only miserable for us, it doesn't help us move forward with our life.

Reflection

Our view of the world is filtered through our own ideas, experiences, beliefs and values. This also applies to our view of other people. The things we like and dislike in others are a reflection of our own unique perception rather than an accurate representation of the person. This is why we each find different things appealing (and unappealing) about a person. If you're struggling with aspects of a person you dislike, consider what this says about you and the things you can learn about yourself. Focusing on your attitude and reaction is likely to be of greater benefit to you; waiting for the other person to change is not.

Giving 100 Percent

We've all had times when there's
been a task we know we have
to do, but which we keep putting
off. A common reason for such
procrastination is that we know
it's going to be difficult or require
100 percent of our concentration.
It's far easier to find other tasks that
don't require such a commitment, and
we can easily fill in our time without
completing the one task we know has
to be done. We're best to get on and
complete the job. Once it's finished
we'll feel really good — and we won't
have to think about it again.

Order

There are times when our life seems to be out of control. We become so busy that we let slip the simple things and once these build up, life can begin to feel chaotic. We look around us and see that the most basic chores are not being completed and the mess is building up. This level of disorder is likely to create a feeling of stress when we're feeling really busy. It's important to dedicate some time to getting our environment in order. Once we have order around us, it's easier to think in an orderly manner and then regain control of what we have to do.

Children

While it might seem we're raising our offspring to be 'good' children, we're really raising them to be effective and contributing adults. How we let our children treat us will be how they treat others in their life. If we let them speak to us or treat us with disrespect, where are they going to learn about respecting others? The same goes for courtesy and trust. If we don't tell them how they make us feel when they treat us inappropriately, how are they going to learn empathy for others? What we expect from our children today will translate into their standards of behaviour tomorrow.

Tolerance

Some of us have the luxury of being able to focus on improving ourselves mentally and spiritually. However, not everyone has the time or the inclination to think about their life in this way and we need to be tolerant of these people. It might be that their focus is on how they can afford to feed and house their families or they might be dealing with issues that threaten their security. There is a basic hierarchy of needs and some people's time and energy are spent on their most basic requirements.

Perfection

If you are a perfectionist you're likely to feel frustrated, irritated and dissatisfied much more than a person who is easy-going. It's hard to achieve perfection some of the time, so attempting to achieve it all of the time is only setting yourself and others up to fail. It's great to have high standards because they lift performance, but reacting negatively to the non-achievement of such high standards will inevitably bring unhappiness to you and those around you.

Material Wealth

A lot of people strive to have more material wealth in their lives because they believe this will make them happy. Yet there are many examples of wealthy people who are not happy and 'poor' people who are happy. Happiness doesn't come from what we have; it comes from who we are, from the way we think about our life, and from our attitude to the things that happen to us. If we strive for happiness rather than material wealth, we're not only more likely to achieve it, but we'll probably find that we don't need increased material wealth at all.

Battles

How often have we felt like doing battle with our children? There are many times when they do not do what we want them to do, or they do something in a way that we consider unsatisfactory. Rather than battling with them all the time, we might pause and ask ourselves whether we should insist that their behaviour matches our wishes and whether a battle is really necessary. On many occasions it is imperative that they do what we want, so think about saving up the battles for those times.

Happiness Envy

As we live our life we may come across people who don't like to see us happy. Our happiness somehow takes away from their happiness. It's important for us to realise that the problem is not ours to own. We are not responsible for another person's happiness – especially if that requires us to look as if we're unhappy, or worse, to avoid happiness in our life because of the effect it has on that person. Our happiness is our responsibility; another person's happiness is their responsibility. We shouldn't inhibit our own happiness just to make someone else feel better.

Being Right

We can't be right all of the time.
We don't know everything, so
there will be times when we believe
something to be the case but it's not.
Our perspective is unique to us, so
sometimes we will interpret situations
incorrectly. If our sense of self-worth
is tied up with being right, far too much
importance will be placed on something
that can't happen all the time.
Moreover, holding onto a position of
righteousness when it's obvious we are
mistaken is likely to reflect negatively
on our integrity. Be real – it's perfectly
acceptable to get it wrong.

Standards

We all have our own standards of behaviour which govern the way we treat people. Different people have different standards, and consequently some people treat others in a way that we don't agree with. Ultimately, the way we treat others largely dictates the way we are treated in return – 'we reap what we sow'. Those who treat others badly are going to experience negative consequences. It's not for us or anyone else to impose our own negative consequences because we disagree with someone else's behaviour. Our negative interference might end up having negative consequences for us!

Giving

The best way to receive is to give. There is a natural balance to everything in life. It's important to keep this in mind if we hope to 'get things' from other people. If we constantly ask for things and we don't give anything in return, the chances of us continuing to get things are reduced. We don't always have to reciprocate at the same level we receive, nor with the same things, but we do need to give something back. Given the natural balance, if a person feels that they are always giving but receiving nothing in return, they will attempt to rectify the imbalance.

Warning

There will be times in life when
we want to warn people about the
negative character traits of others.
However, for many reasons we must
be very careful if we decide to do
this. First, we may have a unique
view of the other person's behaviour.
Secondly, the other person may
demonstrate their negative character
to us alone – possibly because of how
we treat them. Thirdly, it's not good
to be known as a person who talks
disparagingly about others. We're best
to let people decide for themselves
whether or not they like someone, as
this is less likely to rebound on us later.

Inaction

It's not difficult to accept that we must take responsibility for our actions. If our action causes a consequence, we need to take responsibility for that consequence. The same is true for anything we intentionally do not do. If our inaction causes a consequence, we need to take responsibility for that also. In some situations doing nothing creates a negative consequence. If we could have done something to prevent it and we chose not to, the consequence is our responsibility. Our responsibility doesn't apply only when we act; it also applies when we don't act.

Positive Energy

Very rarely will we have positive experiences if we do not behave in a positive manner. People do not respond to negative energy in the same way they respond to positive energy. If we want to have positive experiences yet constantly complain that we never have them, we are unlikely ever to experience them. There may be the odd time when someone will give in to what we want to stop our complaining, but most people are likely to discount our wishes altogether. The breakthrough will only come when we behave in a manner that can be easily reciprocated.

Character Building

We often hear people say that negative experiences are 'character building', and they can be if we think about them in that way. When we face a negative experience, we wish that our life could return to the way it was before, but we have to accept that once we've had any experience we can't go back to the way we were before. Our only option is to move forward. We can move forward taking the positive out of all that happens to us, or we can move forward with residual negativity.

Mistakes

There will be times in our life when we make a mistake – it is part of being human. While we try to avoid making mistakes, they will happen and the key is how we deal with them. Accepting them and learning from them is important. Judging ourselves harshly and continuing to feel bad about making a mistake will negatively impact our ability to live life to the full. Also, judging others for making a mistake is counterproductive – why not support them as they learn from it? As people don't intentionally make mistakes, dwelling on them is not helpful.

Influences

When some people are struggling, they can be comforted by hearing about how others are struggling. Knowing that others are in a similar situation somehow normalises their own experience, while hearing that others are happy and doing well can have the opposite effect. If we're around such people, we can find ourselves talking mainly about what's going wrong with our life as opposed to what's going right. We might feel drained when we come away from them as the negative energy has affected us. While it's important to be supportive of our friends, constantly talking about negative issues is of no real benefit to anyone.

Annoyance

If you find that you're becoming
annoyed at every little thing, the
chances are that your annoyance is
symptomatic of an underlying issue.
If we project our negative feelings on
to every little thing and make every
molehill into a mountain, we're wasting
our energy on matters that are
not the problem. We need to catch
ourselves doing this and before
we launch into a complaint or an
argument, ask ourselves whether the
issue is worthy of such a response.
We'd be better spending our time
dealing with the real issue.

Treating Others

If you're treating someone in a way that you would not like others to find out about, you need to consider whether you should be treating them that way in the first place. While you might think you have a good reason for your actions, chances are you know you are doing something that isn't right, especially if other people knew about it. It can be a good test to use for ourselves. Ideally we should feel good about the way we treat other people – for their benefit and for our own. There is nothing to be gained by treating people badly.

Sincerity

If you say something because it's what you think the other person wants to hear, you're doing both yourself and that person a disservice. By not saying what you really think, you're doing yourself a disservice because you're not being true to yourself in your dealings with others. You're doing the other person a disservice because they don't want to hear you say something you don't mean. They are likely to believe you, and to find out otherwise could cause problems. Hearing the truth is likely to be more acceptable than a message that lacks sincerity.

Bullying

If there's someone in your life who
is trying to belittle or pick on you,
chances are they're unhappy within
themselves. They're trying to ensure
your level of happiness is the same as
theirs. To see someone happier than
they are is unbearable, so they remedy
the situation by trying to make the
other person feel unhappy too.
The trick is not to let these people
affect you. The problem is definitely
theirs and there is no need for you to
take what they're saying seriously.
The worse they behave towards you,
the worse they must feel.
Let the problem remain theirs.

Balance

Our life is a constant balance between pleasing others and doing what is right for ourselves. We're conditioned to want to please others, yet at times we have a strong sense of what is right for us. Most of the time we don't have to think about it because what we want corresponds with what others want of us. An internal conflict can arise when our wants do not match those of others. In that situation, do we give in to others or please ourselves? It's always a balance and if we repeatedly favour one at the expense of the other, we will notice the consequences.

Enjoyment Today

When we die we leave our material wealth behind. Whether or not we believe in an afterlife, the fact remains that we are here now to live our life today. Some people don't live life to the full now because their primary focus is on accumulating material wealth for the future. We don't know what the future holds, and while it's important to be prudent with our finances, we need to consider whether it's worth creating ever greater wealth to be enjoyed at some future date. Don't put off all your enjoyment of life; make sure you enjoy today.

Immunity

If we build up our immune system we might not feel the effects of catching a virus. Our body might fight the virus without us feeling poorly.

Or if we do begin to feel poorly, a strong immune system will aid our body to recover quickly. We can build up our immune system in many ways, including the foods we eat and don't eat. Our physical fitness can also have an impact on our ability to overcome colds and flu. The more we do to look after our body at all times, the better equipped it will be to handle the effects of an illness.

Fear

On the 13th of the month, the saying 'we create what we fear' is particularly appropriate if we are superstitious. If you're worried about having a bad day, your attitude could increase the likelihood of it happening. If you expect things to go wrong, the way you conduct yourself and the way you interact with others will be very different than if you expect things to go right. The way you approach your life will be the biggest determinant in any day's happenings. So rather than worrying about the 13th, use it to consciously adopt a positive attitude.

Feeling Good

Some people live their lives as though they've got a lot to prove. We are our own harshest critic and much of what we strive for in our life is done in order to feel good about who we are. If we don't feel good about ourselves, we may attempt to do bigger and better things in the hope that we'll have a better self-image as a result. While this may happen, we need to realise that a positive sense of self not only comes from what we achieve but also from how we live our daily life.

Injustice

There will be times in our life when we feel as though we've been hard done by. You might be entitled to something you did not receive or you may feel as though you have been treated unjustly. Under these circumstances it can be very tempting to want to take issue and put things 'right'. However, we must consider the cost to ourselves of doing so. Is it worth putting something right, if it means we suffer or lose in the process — whether it be our time, energy or money? Some things are just not worth the battle.

Work Days

Starting work after a holiday can feel very de-motivating. This is because our days on holiday feel very different from our days at work, and we tend to enjoy holidays more than we enjoy working. However, it is possible to make our work days more pleasurable if we choose. For example, we might change what we do before or after we go to work, or it might be possible to change something within our work day. While it's normal to feel de-motivated on returning to work, it doesn't mean you can't improve the way you spend your work days if you choose.

Confidence

Confidence is a state of mind.
If we're confident, we have a belief
system that supports the feeling
that we can handle what we need to
do in life and whatever comes our way.
This belief system might have been in
place for some time because of what
has happened in the past.

However, it's possible to establish
such a belief system now. To gain
confidence we need to behave
confidently and show ourselves that
we can do so. Once we have done this
for a period of time, our belief system
will adjust and as well as behaving
confidently, we will really feel it too.

Deceit

When people are deceitful or speak untruths they generally do so believing they will not be caught.

The consequences of being caught are usually negative. They believe they will not be caught based on what they currently know — yet there is much going on around us that we don't know about, and this can cause outcomes different from those we expect.

The obvious way to ensure this doesn't happen is to live your life honestly and with the best of intentions.

If you do not, understand that you do not know everything nor can you control everything.

Support

When someone else is going through
a tough time it can be difficult to know
how to support them. We might feel we
don't know what to say to make things
better, so we say nothing in
the hope of not making them feel
worse. If we are afraid of feeling
uncomfortable talking to them about
their difficult circumstances, we might
end up not saying anything. Yet at
these times it's our support that is
needed. We don't need to fix their
situation or even try to make things
better; we just need to be there and
be prepared to support irrespective of
how it makes us feel.

Appearance

We all have things about the way we look that we don't like. We tend to focus on these aspects of ourselves and when we look in the mirror we only see our 'faults'. However, we are more than this – we are made up of many features, both internal and external. When others look at us they see a much bigger picture than we do; others generally view us in a more holistic way than we view ourselves. So rather than focusing only on the aspects of yourself that you'd like to be different, balance this out by focusing on aspects of yourself that are great!

Family

Just because we're related to someone doesn't mean we are absolved of putting effort into that relationship. Being someone's parent, brother or sister doesn't automatically mean that you will be trusted, respected or considered supportive – these are things that have to be demonstrated for them to be accepted. It can come as a blow to find out that our relatives don't think of us as we'd like, but if this happens we need to think about how much effort we put in, or whether we take the relationship for granted. Being related will provide a level of tolerance, but it won't ensure an effective relationship.

Contribution

For a relationship to survive, both
parties need to actively contribute
to it. Too often one party withdraws
from the relationship because they
feel their needs are not being met,
yet it can be the withdrawal that puts
the relationship in jeopardy. When
a partner gets caught up in the fact
that their needs are not being met,
they may forget that the very act
of withdrawal can have negative
consequences for the relationship.
So if you have withdrawn from your
relationship, don't assume your partner
will put up with it indefinitely. Rather
than withdraw, deal with the issues
when they arise – before it is too late.

Small Stuff

For most of us our basic survival needs are taken care of, so we have the luxury of only having to concern ourselves about small day-to-day things. If we had to worry about where our next meal was coming from, or where we'd sleep, we wouldn't have time to worry about 'small stuff'. So if you find yourself becoming frazzled by what you have to get done, or what someone else meant by what they said, or how someone else took what you said, consider how lucky you are to be able to think about these matters. This approach will help put the majority of your daily worries into perspective.

Jealousy

To be jealous generally means that we feel someone else has something we'd like – that we're missing out because of what that person has. This can have a profoundly negative effect on us.

In a relationship, jealousy can create the very thing the jealous person is afraid of. Jealousy affects our thoughts and behaviour and can often make us unpleasant to be around.

It can drive others away from us – exactly what we don't want. So be wary of jealousy: it very rarely, if ever, brings about the outcomes we want, and in the process we feel miserable.

Money

It's said that 'money doesn't make people happy', and the people who know this best of all are those with money. Yet the rest of us often think that if we had money we'd be a lot happier than we are now. But while having money would certainly take care of our financial worries, it would also free our minds to worry about other things. If we're worriers, we'll worry no matter what our circumstances. So rather than continually trying to alter your circumstances, take a look at how you can reduce your tendency to worry.

Dread

If you're dreading a situation, consider what it is that you're dreading and why. Know that if you go into a situation with a feeling of dread, you're more likely to have an awful time. In essence it will become a self-fulfilling prophecy. If you figure out why you're dreading it, however, you can then take steps to make the experience more pleasurable. You might need to do something beforehand, or think about the situation in a different way. You can be certain that your attitude to the situation will be the greatest determinant of your own pleasure.

Winding You Up

There will be times when people say something to 'wind you up'. They seem to get some sort of pleasure from your 'wound up' reaction. The best way to stop this sort of thing from happening is to eliminate the source of their pleasure, which is your reaction. If they see that their attempts to wind you up are unsuccessful, they will probably stop – though initially they might try even harder! Also remember that becoming wound up is not beneficial for your wellbeing. So rather than react, stop yourself and avoid the negative impact on your feeling of wellbeing.

Love

Think about something you can do to show a loved one that you love them. It can become too easy to take our loved ones for granted and just get on with our lives trusting that they know we love them. On some level they probably do know that we love them, but an occasional reminder can make a person feel really good. We don't want to end up in a situation where we wish we had done more to show our loved ones how much we loved them. We have the chance now, so make the most of it.

Driving

Why let someone else's driving have a negative impact on you? We've all had moments when our driving deserved a 'toot' from others, but anything more than that would have been unjustified. People don't intend to be bad drivers, so letting ourselves become enraged by such incidents is unnecessary and detrimental. A situation can quickly escalate if aggression is evident, as people can react to it with even more aggression. So rather than feeling angry when you see someone else drive poorly, let it go. It's not worth escalating the incident into a potentially dangerous situation.

Wanting More

If we're comfortable with what we have, or even well off, why do we strive for more and more? Is it greed? One thing to keep in mind is that the quest for more takes time and effort, and might even be problematic. We must consider whether it's worth investing so much energy into something that might not yield us a lot more than we already have. If you already have the means to live a great life, why not start doing so? If you're in this situation you are blessed. Why not put your precious energy into the things in your life that really matter?

Intentions

If you make a decision with the best of intentions, it's hard to have regrets. If you had the best of intentions, what else could you have done? If the decision turned out to have negative consequences, there's probably something for you to learn. It's very easy to focus on the negative consequences and be 'down on yourself' for making a 'wrong' decision, but if you consider what you learned from the experience, was it really wrong? The only way to prevent negative outcomes would be to avoid making decisions, but if we did this we would miss out on life's experiences.

Comfort Zone

It can be tempting to turn down opportunities that take us beyond our comfort zone. If we don't take up the opportunity we will not have to feel the anxiety leading up to it, we will not have to worry about failing and we will not have to think about anything beyond our ordinary experience. While this can be the easy option, we're missing out on an opportunity to extend ourselves and discover what we're capable of. Also, think how fantastic you'll feel if you participate and achieve. Your ability to achieve is only limited by how you think about opportunities, so don't sell yourself short!

Intuition

We often hear people talking about great things happening to them because they were in 'the right place at the right time'. Some opportunities do indeed come along 'out of the blue' and can never be planned for. Yet we tend to spend a lot of our time planning for the future. It can certainly be prudent to plan, but not at the expense of doing what feels right in the moment.

If we do what feels right in the moment, or live intuitively, we're likely to increase our chances of being 'in the right place at the right time'.

Proportion

We've all been in situations where others have had a negative impact on us. It might be as a result of what they said or did to us (or to someone else). It can be easy for us to focus on the impact and think negatively about the person responsible for it, but we should also consider why we let them have such an impact. Why would we let the words and actions of another person have such an impact on the way we feel inside? Why would we then let it consume our thoughts when there are so many positive things we could think about?

Behaviour

Only we know how we feel on the inside, though others can get a sense of it through our behaviour. If we feel inferior around other people, we can mask it by behaving in a way that doesn't show it. If we behave as though we're inferior, we may end up being treated as such, which only perpetuates the original feeling. However, if we behave in a confident manner we'll be treated accordingly. We don't have to be held hostage by our internal thoughts about ourselves. We can change the thought and/or our behaviour to change the reality we experience.

Empathy

It's important to understand the concept of empathy. Empathy is when you put yourself in someone else's shoes and try to imagine what a situation or experience is like for them. Empathising allows you to be effective in your support. What's not effective is for you to take on their burden so that it negatively impacts on you. You have enough to deal with in your own life and, in any case, taking on a burden isn't going to help anyone. The other person needs your support to help them get out of the situation they're in — not for you to jump in there with them.

Potential

We all have within us the power to be truly great and the only thing that gets in the way is our belief about how great we can be. Such beliefs or expectations are only based on what we know and have experienced to date, yet we might end up being great beyond what is currently foreseeable.

If our belief in our potential is limited, we'll miss the opportunities that present themselves and our life will become our own self-fulfilling prophecy. Extend your beliefs so they can encompass any possibility that comes your way.

Needs

A relationship can go awry if either party feels their needs are not being met. If we feel this, we can withdraw from the other person and from the relationship as our inclination to give back is reduced. Yet if this happens the problem will only get worse. A useful exercise for a couple in such a situation is to write down what you need from the other person. You might find the other person has no idea what your needs really are and they've been putting their energy into the wrong things. The fact that your needs are not being met does not mean that the other person hasn't been trying.

Normality

We each have ideas about what is normal and abnormal behaviour. These ideas are fairly narrow, yet they are the rules by which we lead our lives, and if we choose to live by other rules we can feel the pressure of society's judgement.

For example, once it was abnormal to be vegetarian, for a husband to look after the children and for a woman to be the managing director of a large company. If we don't challenge our concepts of what is 'normal' our society will not progress. It is those people whom we currently judge as 'abnormal' who could be leading the way. It's easy to go with the flow; it's much harder to be different.

Lists

Writing a list can help you to order your mind and control what it is you need to do. Once you have your list you can clearly see what needs to be done. You can cross out tasks once completed, thus showing the progress you're making. If a new task crops up, you can include it on your list and decide where it should be inserted. You will easily see how the new task will impact on the other things on your list. Rather than feeling frazzled by what you have to do, write it down, order it and manage it.

Mission Statement

Many companies have a 'mission statement' – a statement that defines what they're trying to achieve by their existence. We too have a purpose in life and it can be helpful to think about a personal mission statement for ourselves. Write a statement about who you are now, then compare it to a statement about what you believe your purpose is. You may find they are quite different. Think about your mission statement, then consider what you need to be doing day to day to ensure your living is consistent with your purpose. If you don't make sure that your behaviour is consistent with your purpose, you will not achieve it.

Motivation

We are all motivated by different things, depending on our beliefs and values, where we are in life, our background and circumstances. What motivates us is likely to change as we move through life. We can't presume to know what motivates another person, nor should we judge them if their motivations are different from our own. Being motivated enables us to achieve more in life, so it helps to know what our motivators are. If we can ensure our motivation, we're more likely to achieve our goals and potential.

Ageing

How often do you look back at yourself in your younger days and wish you were back at that time? Yet consider the things about yourself that you were unhappy with then. While the issues are different from those you're battling today, they were significant and real at the time. The reality is that one day you'll look back on today and wish you were here. Given this, why not enjoy who you are today?

We're just going to keep on getting older, so why not enjoy what you have today rather than pining for what you had 20 years ago?

Fulfilment

We all have a desire to feel fulfilled and most, if not all, of our intentions and behaviours are geared towards achieving this. There are times when we acquire material possessions in the belief that we'll feel fulfilled once we have them. This may happen, but the feeling of fulfilment is very short-lived because material possessions can't truly fulfil us. The way to feel fulfilled is to focus on who you are. Think about what your purpose is and what you can contribute. Creating a positive and healthy sense of yourself is likely to result in true fulfilment; an endless pursuit of material possessions is not.

Last Minute

Leaving things to the last minute can be a recipe for disaster, as we have no idea what challenges we're going to face in the future. If we face a challenge at the very time we are under pressure to complete a task, it can become very stressful. We're also unlikely to complete a task to our normal standard if we're pressured or stressed. So if you have the chance to complete a task ahead of a deadline, do it. If not, do your best to manage any stress you may feel. You will realise the benefit in the quality of the result and your own wellbeing.

Stagnation

Little if any progress will be made
if we constantly think about what
we cannot do. If we're faced with
a problem, it's going to be a long
process to find a solution if we focus
on its downside. This mindset keeps
us stagnant because we never try
anything. Even if we have doubts
about whether a possible solution will
succeed, we must try it or we'll never
know. Also we may find that in the
trying, the real solution will become
obvious. If you're finding that you're
stuck with a problem, consider whether
your thinking is keeping you stagnant.

Patience

Patience is the art of letting something happen in its own time, whereas impatience arises when things don't happen in our time. We don't control everything, and setting expectations around the timing of events can cause frustration because of factors beyond our control. The amount of time something or someone takes is unlikely to be affected by our impatience, so it's futile to be impatient. The only person who truly suffers from the stress of impatience is you, and anyone who happens to be around you at the time. Impatience is something that has been learned, so it can be unlearned.

Hasty Decisions

There will be times in our life when something goes wrong and we'll have a heightened emotional response to it. At these times we typically come up with what we consider to be a solution, yet because of our emotional state the solution may be radical or inappropriate. It's important not to make big decisions when we're emotional because the emotion will eventually subside, but the consequence of our radical decision will remain. Even though the temptation to act seems very strong when we're emotional, it's important to resist it. If it's the right decision, your thinking will not change when your emotions have returned to normal.

Emptiness

If we look to others to fill a void inside ourselves we could be looking for a very long time. It's up to us to complete ourselves, as depending on others for our own fulfilment can lead to problems. For example, the person we come to depend on may one day no longer be in our life. Also, even though it's an impossible task for someone else to complete us, we can be frustrated that it's not happening and unfairly take this out on the person we expect to fill the void. Don't set yourself and others up to fail — your sense of self is your responsibility.

Attitude

Our attitude will influence our internal
wellbeing and have a large bearing
on the success we achieve in life.
To improve our attitude we need to
replace negative or unconstructive
thoughts with positive and constructive
thoughts. This is a simple concept
yet it can be hard to master. First we
need to be able to identify the thoughts
that are not working well for us. Then
we need to catch ourselves having
a negative thought so that we can
replace it with a more positive one.
While it's not always easy, if you really
want to do it, it will happen.

Self-centredness

If those around you are having a bad day, don't automatically assume that it's been caused by something you've done. If we're around someone who is suffering a low mood, it's easy for us to think it's because of us — and then it affects our own thinking and behaviour. For example, we may feel defensive or angry at them for reacting to us in such a way. The reality is that their mood might be due to something else entirely, and in trying to make it about us we will only make matters worse.

Let them be.

Invisible Wall

We do not have to be affected at all
by what others say to us, or say about
us. We cannot control what others
say, but we can control whether
we take it on board or not. One way
to do this is to imagine an invisible wall
between yourself and others.
You control what happens on your side
of the wall, including how you feel.
The only way someone else can have
an effect on you is if you let their
words penetrate your wall. However,
you can choose to allow their words
to ricochet off the wall and have no
impact on you whatsoever.

Fitness

We are bombarded by commercials showing us how we can become fitter and healthier by purchasing various products and services, yet it's possible for us to be fit and healthy without any of them. We have within us the ability to eat well: we don't need fancy regimes and fad diets. We have within us the ability to get physically fit: we don't need fancy equipment or expensive gym memberships.

Don't allow yourself to be put off getting fit and healthy because you don't have the advertised 'extras' or the means to acquire them. You can begin to get fit and healthy today with what you already have.

Hindsight

With the benefit of hindsight, it's possible to see why things happened the way they did. Even though at the time we were hoping for a different outcome, with hindsight it's possible to see that the actual outcome was in fact the best possible one for us.

It's important to learn from this so that we do not become stressed by things not going to plan today. We always need to try our best, but if things are happening beyond our control, just let them happen. Have faith today that you'll achieve the best possible outcome – even if it's not the one you expect.

Inner Worth

The person you are on the inside is not
altered by the clothes you wear, the
car you drive or the house you live in.
These things may alter how others
perceive you, but they have no bearing
on what you have to offer as a person.
If others choose to associate with
you, or vice versa, based on these
external symbols, the relationship is
likely to be founded on superficiality.
It's far more fulfilling for all involved to
associate with people who enjoy you
for who you are and the real things
you have to offer.

Assumptions

Be careful when making assumptions about what people are going to do. We tend to make such assumptions based on what they have done in the past, or what we think we'd do under the same circumstances. However, people change and everyone is different so our chances of making a correct assumption are slim. While it may be helpful at times to consider what someone might do, it's important we don't come to depend on the accuracy of our assumptions, as doing so may only lead to our own frustration and embarrassment.

Key Decisions

Live your life for you, not anyone else.
At times you may feel under pressure
to make major life decisions because of
the wishes of significant others. While
it may end up making them happy,
is it worth it if you end up miserable?
Other people don't walk in our shoes
and they don't live our life day to day,
so making decisions that will affect our
daily life solely to please others may
be to our detriment. Your life is yours
to live, just as it's up to your significant
others to live their lives.

Reading v Action

Reading about something is not going to make it happen. For example, your self-esteem is not going to rise merely by reading about how to increase it — you have to practise the suggestions you're given. As it's much easier to read than it is to put things into practice, some people find themselves going from book to book in search of answers. The only way to make a real difference in your life is to start practising the things you read about and believe in. It may not be easy or happen overnight, but keep practising.

Withdrawal

In our relationships, a common reaction to feeling that your needs are not being met is to withdraw your own effort. Yet doing this is likely to make existing problems greater and it could create others. One way to boost the chances of your needs being met is to increase the effort you put into the relationship. We tend to reciprocate the behaviour we're shown, so rather than making the situation worse and having your lack of effort reciprocated, why not increase your effort and show more of what you'd like in return? We're more likely to receive if we give.

Pay-offs

Your behaviour reflects the belief system you have about yourself. If you think you're a decent person worthy of good things happening to you, you will approach your days with this attitude, and more often than not you will accept nothing less. However, if you think you're a bad person who doesn't deserve good things, you'll approach your days with a negative attitude and again, accept nothing less.

The consequences or 'pay-offs' you achieve reinforce your belief system — whether it's positive or negative. So if you are achieving negative 'pay-offs', you need to alter your belief system.

Reminders

When we are trying to make changes in our life, whether to our diet, exercise, thinking or behaviour, we will experience difficulty if we forget to do things differently as we go about our normal daily routine. Going about our daily activities in our typical automatic fashion will not change anything, so if you're trying to make positive changes in your life, think of things you can do to remind yourself. For example, change your routine, or write down your goals and affirmations and leave them in places where you can see them. Making changes occurs in the moment – it's no use remembering about them later.

Excessive Analysis

Spending too much time 'in our head' analysing a situation can be a waste of time. If there's something you need to figure out, do so by obtaining the facts and focusing on them. The best way to do this is to talk to the people involved.

If you don't do this and spend your time making assumptions based only on what you think you know, you're likely to come to the wrong conclusion. It's easier to spend time 'in your head', but if you want to reach the correct conclusion it pays to work with facts rather than perceptions.

Crisis

When we hit crisis-point we generally have no choice but to take action to rectify the situation. It may take the crisis to motivate us to make the changes we've really known for some time were necessary. While crises are unpleasant, they can serve as a catalyst for change and to this extent we may look back on a crisis and view it positively, as it enabled us to see and make the most of opportunities that we would not otherwise have noticed. In the middle of a crisis it's difficult to see things clearly, but in time you may look back and see it as a positive step in your life.

Food

We need food for energy so we can live our life. However, for some of us food plays a different role and we need it for other reasons – perhaps to feel safe and secure, or as a reward for hard times. If we eat food for reasons other than to fuel our bodies, we may end up eating more than is required and suffer the consequences. If you find that you're eating more food than your body needs to function, consider what other roles food plays in your life. If you can find fulfilment by other means, your need for extra food may diminish.

Burnout

If you feel that you're losing your ability to cope and may be about to 'burn out', it's worth asking for help. While you might not want to do this for fear of being an inconvenience or worrying what people will think of you, it's far better to prevent yourself from burning out if possible. If you were to burn out, you would definitely require the assistance of others to be able to function on a day-to-day basis. If you consider it a burden to ask for help now, how would you cope with the level of assistance required once you had burnt out? Prevention is far better for you and for those around you.

Honesty

If someone asks you what you would like to do, what you would like to eat or what gift you would like, don't be afraid to say what you want.

If they're asking you, it's because they want to know. If they don't want to know, they shouldn't ask. If you say something just to be polite, they may feel as though they're giving you what you want – but you end up being disappointed, and that's not fair to them. If you say what you want and it's not possible for some reason, that's fine, but at least everyone's being honest.

One Thought

We only have the ability to think about one thing at a time. While we may have many things on the go at once, we can only have one thought in our mind at any moment. What we spend our time thinking about is important because it takes up valuable thinking time, has an effect on the way we feel and can have a real influence on our daily life. Given this, it's important to try and make sure that the majority – if not all – of our thoughts are positive. We will certainly benefit in all aspects of our life if we do so.

Two-faced

Do you have someone in your life whom you don't like very much but you try to be nice to when you need something from them? Behaving one way while thinking another can create an internal conflict for you, as well as a loss of respect from the other person. If there are going to be times when you need something from someone you don't care for, is it not worth trying to foster a more effective relationship with them? Or if this is not possible, it might be worth finding a situation where you don't need anything from them. Being 'two-faced' does not benefit anyone.

The Worst

Imagining the worst is a habit that serves to prepare us for the worst eventuality. We feel that if we're prepared for the worst, the impact when it comes will somehow be lessened as we've already thought about how we'd handle things.

The reality is that the worst might not happen, and if it does it's unlikely to happen exactly as we imagined.

Also, if all of your focus is on the worst outcome, it might increase the chances of it happening. Better to have a state of mind that enables you to deal with whatever comes your way, and spend your energy in this moment focusing on something positive.

Desperately
Seeking ...

Have you noticed that the more
desperate you are for something to
happen, the less likely it is that it will?
There may be many reasons for this.
For example, you focus your attention
on the desperation rather than doing
what you can to achieve the outcome
you want. Also, the more you focus
on not having something, the more
you notice it — and it can then feel
like an eternity before you get it. It's
as though we send out a 'desperate
energy' that repels the very thing we
believe we need. The key is to avoid
becoming desperate. If something is
meant to happen, it will.

Put-downs

There are many reasons why others may try to put us down. Some are intentional and some are not, but none has anything to do with us. It can be difficult to maintain this perspective in the moment, and it's easy for us to believe what we're being told – especially if someone we love is telling us. Even though we love someone and they love us, they may still feel threatened by us in some way or get their sense of self from feeling they're better than us. Irrespective of their issues, it is unacceptable for them to put us down.

Revenge

When we have intentionally been treated badly by another person, it's common for us to want to make the other person feel bad also — or exact revenge. The problem with revenge is that it consumes us and prolongs the bad feelings we have. Moreover, if someone hurts us intentionally, they're very unlikely to be happy themselves, so why focus our precious effort and energy on making them even more unhappy? Focusing on the negative only brings about more negativity, so we're better to let it go and focus on making our life the best we can.

In Control

A controlling person tends to be someone who thinks they know best. Rather than let things be and see what outcome eventuates, a controlling person likes to ensure a particular outcome no matter what. The risk with this approach is that we don't always know what's best as we can never know everything. We can only judge a situation on the basis of the information and experience we have to date. Therefore, if we give up total control but continue to try our best, we may achieve an outcome that is beyond what we could ever expect.

Interaction

If you're unhappy with the way another person interacts with you, the best thing you can do to change the situation is to alter the way you interact with them. When two people interact, both parties influence the dynamic and have an effect on the interaction. Even though you may think you're being neutral and the problem is solely with the other person, they will be interpreting your behaviour and responding accordingly. If you change your behaviour so that it more closely resembles what you'd like in return, their response to you is likely to be different.

Conviction

If you really want something to happen, you'll make it happen. If you think you really want something to happen but it's not happening, there will be a reason for it. You will be getting a pay-off by leaving things the way they are. The pay-off is likely to be reinforcing a belief you have about yourself. For example, if you're not eating right and exercising, it may be because you believe that you're lazy and not worthy of feeling good. The belief can be adjusted by changing your thinking or taking action to the contrary. Be the master of your life.

Positive or Negative

On balance, do you think positively or negatively about things? If something happens, do you put a positive or negative spin on it? Do you react to news compassionately or do you look for the 'gossip value' you can get out of it? The way we think is largely habitual and has a significant impact on our day-to-day experiences. If you discover that you're a mainly negative thinker, this may be impacting on your experiences without your really knowing it. If you make a conscious choice to change to more positive thinking, it's likely to have a positive impact on your life.

Being Direct

If we're not prepared to be direct with people about what we want or need, we shouldn't be frustrated with them for not providing it. Some of us prefer other people to be able to work out what it is we want or need and provide it without having to spell it out. Yet would you rather be charged with the responsibility of trying to figure out someone else's needs, then be persecuted for getting it wrong, or be told directly so that you have a chance of getting it right? Set your relationships up to succeed rather than fail.

Self-criticism

If you judge yourself harshly for the way you've behaved in the past, what are you doing now that shows you've learned from that?

It's a waste of time thinking and feeling bad about what you've done in the past as you can't change it. Once you've said or done something, you cannot take it back. The key is to prevent a similar situation from occurring again. To do this you might need to consider the possible consequences of your actions, and if there's a chance you might regret saying or doing something, weigh up whether it's worth proceeding.

Out Of Control

If we have too much on the go at once, it may feel as though we're out of control. This feeling is not beneficial to us or the people around us. Feeling out of control can lead to outbursts, stress and ultimately burnout. It is better for everyone if we keep our daily activities at a manageable level. This may mean dropping something out of your daily routine that is not necessary, or not running your children to so many activities. The most important thing we can do is to remain healthy in body and mind.

Ups And Downs

We all go through ups and downs.
When we're in a relationship we go
through our own 'down' times and
witness our partner going through
theirs. The key is not to get enmeshed
in the other person's 'downs'. When
our partner's mood is down it can
be easy for us to take it personally,
either by thinking we are the cause
of it, or by feeling sorry for ourselves
that we're having to put up with it.
However, we will also go through
'down' times, and what we'd like
is some compassion, tolerance and
space. It's all about treating others as
we would like to be treated ourselves.

Comparisons

There may be times when it is useful to compare our problems with those other people are experiencing. Such an exercise may help put our problems in perspective and make us feel better. However, it's important to realise that the problem itself doesn't cause a person to suffer, it's how the problem affects them. For example, one person could be dealing with the death of their spouse and another person could be dealing with the death of their cat, yet the experience may be equally real and unbearable for each of them. We must be careful not to judge others based on their reactions to problems in their life.

Something For Nothing

We very rarely get something for nothing. If you're expecting to receive something from another person, the best way to ensure you get it is by giving yourself. This doesn't mean you have to buy gifts to receive gifts, but you might like to think of putting in an effort with that person. Do you call them to find out how they are or do you just call them when you want something? Most people don't take kindly to being taken for granted, but usually respond very kindly to genuine effort. So consider whether it is reasonable to have expectations of people who don't receive your genuine effort.

Self-esteem

Our self-esteem is dependent on the value we place on the attributes we have. Too often we look at the attributes of others and wish we had them ourselves. We then believe that because we don't have those attributes we're not the best we can be, so we begin to feel negatively about ourselves. We focus on what we don't have at the expense of what we do have. But it's more than likely that someone out there is looking at us wishing they had what we have! Rather than always focusing outwards, try focusing inwards and notice the effect on your self-esteem.

Receiving

Some people say, 'I'd rather give than receive a gift.' The act of giving certainly makes a person feel good, but if we are on the receiving end and do not respond appropriately, the giver's pleasure will be minimised. If we communicate our feelings of guilt around accepting the gift, perhaps requiring the giver to justify their reasons for giving it to us, we're likely to detract from their experience of giving, thus creating a 'no-win' situation. The best thing we can do when receiving a gift is to say, 'Thank you, you are very kind.'

Live Your Life

How much time do you actually have with nothing to do, when you can just enjoy your day? How much time do you spend on the go, believing you always have something that needs to be done? The difference between these two questions is whether or not you are living your life or just working your way through it. Allowing yourself to live your life will benefit you on all levels. Letting go all that needs to be done and doing what you really want to do can have a tremendously rejuvenating effect. There will always be something that needs to be done, but we will never get this day again.

Relationships

The best relationships are those in which each partner lets the other grow. The key to this is letting our partners do what they need to do for themselves, with or without us. It might be spending time by themselves or doing something that we wouldn't enjoy. Making changes of this kind could make us feel afraid because they take us away from our familiar way of life. However, if each partner is allowed to grow and develop as an individual, then the change will only bring about a positive outcome for all. By letting a partner grow, they will be able to contribute more to the relationship.

Support Network

It's important to have a network of people in our lives who we can count on for different things. Each person has strengths and weaknesses and can contribute to our lives in a different way. The problem arises when we look to one person to fulfil all our needs. It's very difficult for one person to be our 'everything', and if we expect them to be, we're jeopardising our relationship with them and setting them up to fail. People do their best with what they have to offer, and rather than wanting them to provide us with more, we should be grateful for what they can give us.

Dance

It's very hard to dance and not be present in the moment.

It's also hard to dance and feel unhappy. We often forget about dancing as an option to make us feel good – especially if we're only used to dancing at parties or clubs. Yet dancing alone may produce the most fun, as we don't have to worry about our dancing style. All we need is a piece of music we like. Taking time out to dance is rejuvenating, uplifting and excellent exercise. So remember dancing as an option when you need some cheering up.

Happy Household

Children deserve to live in a happy household. While there will be times when parents have issues to work through, this doesn't mean that the household needs to descend into chaos. Issues can be discussed and resolved in an amicable manner, but both parties need to be willing to do so. This extends to situations where parents are divorced or separated.

Showing a willingness to relate amicably to your ex-partner will have a positive effect on your children, your relationship and your family – so why would you do anything else?

Hormones

Each of us is affected by our hormones. There will be times when our hormones seem to urge us to behave in ways we'd otherwise consider inappropriate. At these times we have to rely on logical thinking and common sense to make the right choices. In the heat of the moment it always seems easiest to go with how we're feeling, but if this results in an unfavourable outcome, we have to try hard to do something different. Doing the right thing does take effort, and hormones can provide an excellent excuse to do the contrary, but we will still have to live with the consequences.

Frustration

We can become frustrated if things don't happen within the timeframe we'd like – especially if we're not in control. However, in these situations we may be being given an opportunity to learn something about ourselves. It may be learning patience; it may be learning how to deal with frustration; it may be learning to be contented when we're not in control. Everything happens for a reason and for our greatest good, so rather than feeling negative, consider what you could be learning and have faith that all will turn out for our best.

Communication Styles

We all have different styles of communicating. Some people provide only the facts while others like to provide the context surrounding the facts. Some people only speak truths while others like to embellish their communications to add appeal and interest. There's no point spending time delivering context or embellishing our story if the person we're talking to only wants facts. If you find it difficult communicating with a particular person, consider how you might alter your style to ensure they get your message. Understanding our own and others' communication styles helps us communicate more effectively.

Objectivity

We may find it easier to look at someone else's life and have an opinion on how they should fix their problems than know what we should do to fix our own. It can be difficult to see our own situation with objectivity. Objectivity removes the emotion that we have tied up with certain behaviours and outcomes in our own life. Having said that, while an objective perspective may be useful, it will always be up to us to make the changes necessary to bring our life back on track.

Symptoms

Our body is great at signalling to us that all is not well. These signs can be different from person to person, and it's important that we each understand our body well enough to know when it's giving us a signal to change something we're doing. If your body is showing abnormality or distress, it might pay to look at how you're living your life. Are you pushing yourself too much? Are you not eating healthily? Are you suffering emotionally? It pays to deal with the cause of these symptoms before they turn into something that is very difficult to overcome.

Resisting Temptation

To achieve a goal, we often have to resist immediate temptation. We typically fail to do this because of two major hurdles. First, we rationalise that giving into temptation on this one occasion isn't going to make much difference. Secondly, we forget about the ultimate goal we're trying to achieve when faced with the temptation. But if we give in once, we're likely to do it again, and it's important to take steps to ensure we don't forget the ultimate goal. We could write it down and carry it around or wear something symbolic to remind us. If we're truly dedicated, we'll do what it takes to achieve success.

Perseverance

There is a saying: 'If at first you don't succeed, try and try again.' Perseverance is critical to achieving our goals in life. However, if we find that we're not achieving the desired outcome through a particular approach, we should consider changing the approach. Someone defined insanity as 'trying the same thing over and over while expecting a different result.' So persevere, but try changing your approach if you're not successful in your attempts at achieving your goal. If you continue to be unsuccessful, you might consider whether the outcome you're striving for is right for you.

Hard Times

All relationships have hard times.
How we deal with them will determine
the success of our relationship.
Overcoming hard times takes
commitment and dedication from both
parties. If one party withdraws from
the other, this may have a detrimental
effect. Even though what we're facing
may seem difficult to overcome, with
a calm and supportive approach most
things can be worked through.
It certainly doesn't make sense to
end a relationship based on hard
times, as they will be present in all
relationships we have. Focus your
energy on how best to work through
the problem facing you.

The Driving Seat

Each of us is in control of our own life. If there's something in our life that isn't working, it's up to us to change it. We are not in control of others' lives, so it's risky to rely on them to make changes so that aspects of our life work well: why should they? If they do, it's because they choose to at that time. They could easily make another choice or postpone it indefinitely. Accepting and embracing the power and control we have in our own life means we're more likely to achieve our potential.

Unconditional Love

The relationship we have with our children is like no other. We love our children no matter what, which is the definition of unconditional love. Our ability to love unconditionally is our greatest gift and one we should recognise within ourselves. Being able to love another unconditionally benefits our soul, for loving without expectation is the purest love of all.

The ultimate would be to love everyone in our lives unconditionally. We tend to let the behaviour of others put us off loving them unconditionally. Every soul is worthy of unconditional love and capable of giving it.

Escape

If we're not happy within ourselves we may attempt to escape the feeling by wanting to be anywhere but where we are now. The problem with this is that when we end up in our new setting, we'll still have our unhappiness. It can sometimes take considerable effort to change our circumstances, and it can be very disheartening to find out that in the end the change hasn't 'worked' for us. Rather than focusing on a change of setting to deal with your unhappiness, focus on the unhappiness. If you can be happy here, you can be happy anywhere.

Diet

To feel good we need balance in all things, including the food we eat. Food has an impact on the chemicals in our body, which in turn affect the way we feel. If we eat too much processed food, for example, the unnatural chemicals can cause an internal imbalance and alter our sense of wellbeing. It's important that we eat a balanced diet and avoid too many sugary or high-caffeine drinks. If you notice that you're not feeling 100 percent (both mentally and physically), consider whether your diet — both food and drink — is balanced.

Changing Tactics

If someone is getting on our nerves it can be tempting to 'put them down' for what they're doing. In putting them down, we hope they'll stop the behaviour we don't like. Yet from their perspective, continually being put down has a negative effect on the way they feel about themselves and about us. We're more likely to achieve the outcome we want if we're with a happy person. So rather than making the person feel bad, which won't work, why not think about what they need to feel good? It's worth a shot.

Independence

It's good to feel needed – it can provide us with a sense of worth. It's therefore possible to understand why someone might foster and maintain a situation where they are needed by another person. There will be times in our life when we are needed by others to help them through difficult times, but it can become unhealthy for one person to be continually dependent on another for something they could and should get from themselves. Enabling someone else to become independent is a great gift and certainly shouldn't detract from the way we feel about ourselves.